Them

Samah Sabawi

CURRENCY PRESS
The performing arts publisher

CURRENT THEATRE SERIES

First published in 2021
by Currency Press Pty Ltd,
PO Box 2287, Strawberry Hills, NSW, 2012, Australia
enquiries@currency.com.au
www.currency.com.au

Copyright: *Them* © Samah Sabawi, 2019, 2021.

COPYING FOR EDUCATIONAL PURPOSES

The Australian *Copyright Act 1968* (Act) allows a maximum of one chapter or 10% of this book, whichever is the greater, to be copied by any educational institution for its educational purposes provided that that educational institution (or the body that administers it) has given a remuneration notice to Copyright Agency (CA) under the Act.

For details of the CA licence for educational institutions contact CA, 11/66 Goulburn Street, Sydney, NSW, 2000; tel: within Australia 1800 066 844 toll free; outside Australia 61 2 9394 7600; fax: 61 2 9394 7601; email: info@copyright.com.au

COPYING FOR OTHER PURPOSES

Except as permitted under the Act, for example a fair dealing for the purposes of study, research, criticism or review, no part of this book may be reproduced, stored in a retrieval system, or transmitted in any form or by any means without prior written permission. All enquiries should be made to the publisher at the address above.

Any performance or public reading of *Them* is forbidden unless a licence has been received from the author or the author's agent. The purchase of this book in no way gives the purchaser the right to perform the play in public, whether by means of a staged production or a reading. All applications for public performance should be addressed to the author c/- Currency Press.

Typeset by Dean Nottle for Currency Press.
Cover features Claudia Greenstone, photo by Justyn Koh.
Cover designed by Mathias Johansson for Currency Press.

Currency Press acknowledges the Traditional Owners of the Country on which we live and work. We pay our respects to all Aboriginal and Torres Strait Islander Elders, past and present.

 A catalogue record for this book is available from the National Library of Australia

Contents

THEM   1

Theatre Program at the end of the playtext

For my cousin Lobna, and for all the mothers who desperately search for a place to shelter their babies from the falling bombs.

Them was first produced by Samah Sabawi and Lara Week, in collaboration with La Mama Theatre, at La Mama Courthouse, Melbourne, on 29 May 2019, with the following cast:

LEILA	Priscilla Doueihy
OMAR	Abdulrahman Hammoud
SALMA	Claudia Greenstone
MOHAMED	Reece Vella
MAJID	Khisraw Jones-Shukoor
PIANO MAN	Nahed Elrayes

Director, Bagryana Popov
Set and Costume Designer, Lara Week
Lighting Designer, Shane Grant
Sound Designer, Elissa Goodrich
Design Assistant and Prop Maker, Lara Chamas
Stage Manager, Hayley Fox
Producer, Lara Week

CHARACTERS

LEILA, a young mother in her early 20s, married to Omar

OMAR, Leila's husband, a young father who used to be a school teacher before the school was bombed

MAJID, Omar's friend, a small-built man in his mid 20s

MOHAMED, Omar's best friend. He is in his late 20s and is the leader of the local resistance militia

SALMA, Omar's sister and 'matchmaker'. She's in her late 20s and has a prominent scar on her face

GUARDS 1 and 2, can be played by actors performing the roles of Omar and Majid

PIANO MAN, man in his mid 20s

MARWAN, to be substituted with a baby doll

SETTING

In what was once a quiet neighbourhood, somewhere in the Arab world.

DIVERSITY PLEDGE

I encourage the producer to collaborate with artists from diverse backgrounds in the realisation and presentation of this work.

This play went to press before the end of rehearsals and may differ from the play as performed.

PROLOGUE

Street. Dusty with scattered rocks and debris. There is a piano on the right, three chairs and a sheesha* in the middle and a checkpoint on the left.

As the audience comes into the theatre, the PIANO MAN *is sitting at the piano and playing a lively tune while* MAJID, OMAR *and* MOHAMED *stand next to him, casually singing along or dancing. Once the audience is seated, the sound of an explosion interrupts the music. The men run offstage in a panic. The* PIANO MAN *pushes his piano offstage. Lights go out as the sound of bombing ensues and continues into the next scene.*

SCENE ONE

Bedroom. Lights fade on to a modestly furnished bedroom. There are a few scattered baby toys on the floor. The bombing finally stops and is followed by a moment of silence. LEILA *and* OMAR*'s voices are heard speaking in loud whispers from underneath the bed.*

LEILA: They stopped.
OMAR: About time!

 The sound of the dawn call for prayer is heard.

Dawn is breaking. How is Marwan?
LEILA: [*sighing*] He sleeps whenever the explosions are loud. Here, put your hand on his heart. Can you feel how fast it's beating?
OMAR: Like a horse on a racecourse.
LEILA: I wanna wake him up.
OMAR: No. Let him sleep.

 Pause.

LEILA: I need to get out.
OMAR: No no no no … don't. Not yet.

 Baby Marwan stirs.

Don't move him. He'll wake up.

---

* Also known as a hookah or water pipe

LEILA: So what? Just leave him under the bed?
OMAR: We should all stay under the bed for a few more minutes just to be sure they're done playing with their big guns.
LEILA: I can't. I'm going crazy down here. I've got to get out.
OMAR: [*seductively*] Would a little bit of *this* help convince you to stay? You know, we've never tried it down here before?

Sound of kissing.

LEILA: Oh, please! Really? *It?*

OMAR *laughs lightly.*

Careful. Marwan will wake up.
OMAR: You're right. Let's go somewhere else. Meet me under the left side of the headboard, right next to the slippers.
LEILA: As sexy as your proposition sounds, and I mean what girl in her right mind would say no to a romantic rendezvous next to a pair of slippers, but I'm going to have to decline.
OMAR: You're breaking my heart.

LEILA *crawls out from under the bed.*

Wait! Stay with me.
LEILA: I can't! I need to remind myself I'm human, and not some frightened insect hiding under the furniture.

The baby grizzles.

OMAR: Shhhhhh … you see what you've done? Now he's awake.

LEILA *stands and stretches her arms and legs before she sits down on the floor and leans her back on the bed. She reaches for her phone and starts to scroll on it.* OMAR *follows her and gently pulls the baby out from under the bed. The baby makes a crying noise,* OMAR *stands up and begins to pace the room with Marwan in his arms, gently humming a lullaby.*

LEILA: Omar.
OMAR: Yes.
LEILA: We shouldn't sleep together anymore.
OMAR: [*dramatically*] Woah woah woah. This is all we've got!
LEILA: Can you be serious?
OMAR: Never! It would kill me.
LEILA: Well, you might be killed anyway. We are in the middle of a war.

OMAR: You don't know that. This could be the end of the war.
LEILA: Or it could just be the beginning.
OMAR: All the more reason not to be serious.
LEILA: Let's spread out. Sleep in opposite corners of the apartment, so when a bomb falls—
OMAR: *If* a bomb falls.
LEILA: Fine. So *if* a bomb falls, one of us might still survive …
OMAR: And live to mourn the other …?
LEILA: If I die, Marwan would at least have you.

> *The baby cries,* LEILA *puts her arms out gesturing to* OMAR *to hand him over. She starts to breastfeed the baby while continuing the conversation.* OMAR *sits next to her and looks on with loving eyes.*

OMAR: What if Marwan is with you and I'm the wretched one that survives? I don't want a life that doesn't have you and Marwan in it.
LEILA: We have to increase our chances. For Marwan's sake.
OMAR: I don't have a chance without you. I will sleep with you. Live with you. Die with you. [*Jokingly*] Darling …
LEILA: Yes?
OMAR: Would you be so kind as to share a bomb with me?
LEILA: Not funny.

> LEILA *and* OMAR *grab their mobile phones and scroll quietly for a moment.*

OMAR: You'll be relieved to know, according to the news, the fighting was all in the South.
LEILA: And once again only bad people … terrorists … were killed?
OMAR: Absolutely!
LEILA: Why is that?
OMAR: Because civilians here have a special protective skin. Bombs bounce right off it.
LEILA: Of course!
OMAR: Most of the fighting was literally three streets down from here.

> *Pause.*

LEILA: You know what this means?
OMAR: They're practically at our doorstep.

> LEILA *leans closer to* OMAR, *holding her phone up.*

LEILA: Smile!

They both fake a smile. She snaps a selfie with her phone camera.

OMAR: What was that for?

LEILA: Mama. I messaged her to say we're fine but she demanded proof.

OMAR: Don't post it online. I don't want my friends to see it. They're perverts.

LEILA: With the way I look now, you really shouldn't worry.

OMAR: The way you look? Do you have any idea how beautiful you look?

LEILA smiles tenderly as he gets closer.

Is Marwan sleeping?

LEILA: Not yet. He's still feeding.

OMAR: Man … I swear this kid has it in for me. He only sleeps during the fighting and is wide awake whenever there is calm.

They return to their phones.

LEILA: We should have left with my parents. Look! They posted new photos … they seem so … happy.

OMAR: Everyone smiles in photos. We just did. Doesn't mean they're happy.

LEILA: They're safe. I know that would make me happy.

OMAR: They live off charity in a foreign country in some stranger's home.

LEILA: It's temporary. They'll be settled soon. Look!

She shows him her phone screen.

This is their new neighbourhood. It's so lush and green. Can you imagine Marwan running through this park?

OMAR: *Their* new neighbourhood? *Habibti*, that is not now, nor will it ever be *their* neighbourhood. They will always be made to feel like outsiders there. Besides, their old neighbourhood used to be green too.

LEILA: Not anymore. Everything here is now so grey, even the trees are now coated with layers of ash, rubble and dust.

OMAR: Things will go back to how they used to be. Remember how your parents used to invite us every Friday?

LEILA: Ahhh … the smell of my mother's fresh bread.

OMAR: And your father' secret falafel recipe.

LEILA: He was so proud of his falafels he almost disowned my brother once for saying it needed more salt.
OMAR: The smell of mint tea on the balcony.
LEILA: Watching children play in the street ...
OMAR: Mmmm ... and eating sweets from Abu Abdo's bakery ...
LEILA: Abu Abdo left. He is selling sweets to strangers in Europe now.
OMAR: They'll never appreciate him the way we did.
LEILA: I miss them.
OMAR: It will be over soon. Things will return to the way they used to be.

OMAR gently kisses LEILA's hand.

LEILA: Omar. Please. Ask Mohamed.
OMAR: Since when do I need Mohamed's permission to kiss you?
LEILA: About leaving. Ask him about leaving. I'm sure he knows some people who can help us get to the coast. Once there we can get on the boat.
OMAR: I told you I have no intention of catching a deathtrap.
LEILA: And this? This is not a deathtrap?
OMAR: This is our home. We just have to wait things out.
LEILA: Wait things out? Till when?
OMAR: My parents lived their entire life wishing they never left their village.
LEILA: This is different.
OMAR: They said the only road to take from here was the one that leads back home.
LEILA: Your parents lived and died refugees. Is this what you want for us? We've got to get out.
OMAR: And what do you think we'll be when we leave? We'll still be refugees. If we survive the trip without getting killed, if we make it through the borders without getting herded into a refugee camp with razor wire and guard dogs, if we make it to the coast alive and get on a boat, if the boat doesn't sink on the way and we actually make it to safety, what do you think we'll be? [*Yelling*] Refugees!
LEILA: If and if and if ... Some refugees become citizens. So don't give me your ifs.
OMAR: Citizens? Even if we become citizens, we will always be outsiders. It will never be home.
LEILA: Just keep an open mind. Please ask Mohamed. Please!

OMAR: I don't trust his judgment. One day he is fighting with the rebels, the next day he is with the army calling the rebels traitors.
LEILA: Things have been confusing. But he is powerful and well-connected.
OMAR: He is full of shit. Why don't we just wait? Look here, the BBC says the UN has struck a deal and the siege will be lifted tomorrow, so aid will get through.
LEILA: This is just another cycle and you know it. What do you think will happen the day after tomorrow? The camp resistance cannot hold for much longer. Soon they will march in here and occupy us.
OMAR: Who? Who will occupy us?
LEILA: They. *Them.*
OMAR: Which *them*?
LEILA: Any *them* … Be it them who kill in the name of God, or them who massacre in the name of democracy, or them in the sky claiming civility while dropping barrel bombs … all of them … any of them.
OMAR: When the time comes I will fight to defend my home and my family. I will not run away.
LEILA: [*sarcastically*] You? You will fight?
OMAR: Yes.
LEILA: [*laughing*] You will hold a rifle and kill?
OMAR: No, I'm not a fan of rifles. I'm more of an RPG type. They have far more sex appeal. Also I find that their rustic tone brings out the colour in my eyes.
LEILA: You've never killed anything in your life.
OMAR: How hard can it be?
LEILA: I'm pretty sure it's harder than killing a lamb.
OMAR: Seriously? You're bringing that up now? In front of my son?
LEILA: Yes. We're the only ones who never slaughtered a lamb on Eid. I ran out of excuses to explain to the neighbours why my husband can't get himself to slaughter a lamb.
OMAR: I respect them too much.
LEILA: You respect lambs.
OMAR: Yes. They don't have any imperial interests, they don't claim to speak for God, and they never fight in proxy wars.

His phone rings. He looks at the number and seems surprised.

It's Salma.

LEILA: Well … go on!
OMAR: Do I really have to?
> *He picks up the call.*

Hello, sis! How are you? [*Smiling tenderly*] Yeah, good to hear your voice too … What do you mean you're coming back? … Are you crazy? … No. No. No-one comes back … It's not safe and we … Yes … I know the UN will open a safe corridor but … Salma, listen to me, it's better for you to stay where you are … Trust me, you don't want to be … Of course, we're fine. No, I said we're fine. Don't … no … don't come here … Yes, we miss you but … Fine. Sure. Okay. Yes. Whatever. What? … Mohamed? The nerve you have? … You want Mohamed to help you? … Mohamed? After what you did to him? You … you don't even feel remorse, do you? Oh, what's the point? Sure … I will ask him to wait for you at the checkpoint. Will you be coming on the bus or riding on your broom?

> LEILA *nudges him with her elbow.*

Safe travels, sis!

> *He hangs up and is visibly irritated …*

Urghhhh …!
LEILA: Salma is coming?
OMAR: Like an inevitable storm. She'll be here tomorrow. I don't understand why she is so—urghhh … she never listens to me.
LEILA: It will be good to see her. To have family here.

> OMAR *looks at* LEILA *with suspicion.*

OMAR: You knew.
LEILA: What?
OMAR: You knew she was coming?
LEILA: I knew she was thinking of coming. She misses us. She wanted to see Marwan … and the UN will open a safe corridor for people to pass … this time they negotiated for it to remain open for three days … this way people can get in … and out …
OMAR: Yeah, well most people get out, they don't get *in*.
LEILA: See! You agree. We should get out too.
OMAR: Don't change the subject. What did you tell Salma?
LEILA: Nothing. Only that we miss her.

OMAR: Oh no. Leila, no. Don't lie to me. I can tell when you lie to me. Your chin trembles.

LEILA: It does not.

> OMAR *stares at her. She tries to hide her chin.*

OMAR: Aha! Got you. There it is! I knew you were lying. What did you tell her? Did you ask her for help?

LEILA: We *do* need help. And I don't have to tell her anything. She watches the news. We've been bombed so many times, it is not a secret that we *need help*.

OMAR: Not her help. When she gets here, you need to make sure she behaves. We should probably put her on a leash. She is like a vulture. She preys on the most desperate women.

LEILA: She does not!

OMAR: Why are you defending her?

LEILA: She is your sister. She is Marwan's only aunty and the only family we have left. Everyone else is either dead or gone.

OMAR: Yeah, well … I wish she was dead or—

LEILA: [*interrupting*] Omar. Don't.

OMAR: And that money she keeps flashing around … it's like poison.

LEILA: So what if she found a way to make money in this miserable war.

OMAR: By selling our little girls to the highest bidder?

LEILA: She's not *selling* and they are not *little*. She brokers marriages to young women. She helps them, and yes, she helps put food on our table.

OMAR: We don't need her help.

LEILA: Omar, we spent weeks eating nothing but grass and herb soup.

OMAR: So now you're too good for my grass and herb soup? I'll have you know, I only pick the freshest grass in the field for you. Our neighbour Om Fahmy was so jealous the other day when she smelled the aroma of our fresh grass soup she nearly divorced her husband.

LEILA: Everything is a joke to you.

OMAR: Not everything.

LEILA: Everything. And guess what? Your jokes will not save us.

OMAR: Maybe not, but they put a smile on your face … and that is all I need to survive.

LEILA: What's the point of putting a smile on my face when all I can eat is grass? I'd rather be crying over a juicy steak.

OMAR: You are ungrateful.
LEILA: *You* are ungrateful. *We* should be on our knees thanking God Salma is on her way. Her *poison money* will keep Marwan alive … not your sense of humour.
OMAR: So you're saying I've failed to provide for you and Marwan and now Salma will come and make everything okay?
LEILA: That's not what I said.
OMAR: No, that's exactly what you meant.
LEILA: Don't twist my words.
OMAR: I'm not twisting your words. I hear you clearly. I promise, no more jokes. From now on, I'll be serious. So here is my serious outlook on the situation: Yes my dear, you are so clever to have worked this out. It is true; this place is a deathtrap. Yes, we are all doomed so we can sit and wait until we are dead, and while we wait, we must be serious and we must find no reason to enjoy even those precious moments we have together … because God forbid that we should forget for one minute *there's a fucking war going on.*
LEILA: I'm sorry.

Silence. OMAR, *angry, looks away.*

I'm sorry. Come on … you are taking good care of us. You are. Don't be upset.
OMAR: Upset? I am not upset, *this* is my serious face.
LEILA: Your serious face sucks. Come on … did I ever tell you how much I love eating the grass you bring? Just imagining you in the field elbowing our neighbour Abu Fahmy out of your way as you reach for the freshest greenest bunch … makes me … so … hot …

OMAR *continues to look serious and ignores* LEILA.

Okay. Fine. Don't pay me any attention. Just ignore me.

She gently puts the baby on a blanket next to the bed.

That's too bad for you … really … because Marwan has finally fallen asleep.
OMAR: Screw being serious. I'm over it.

LEILA *giggles as* OMAR *enthusiastically pulls a blanket from the bed and throws it over them. They start to move under the blanket. The sound of firing resumes.* LEILA *comes out from under the blanket, followed by* OMAR.

Come back. Let's just keep going. Ignore them.
LEILA: You know I can't. If we get killed, do you not care if they find us in a compromised position?
OMAR: We'll be dead. I don't care how they find us. It won't matter.
LEILA: Well, I care. I don't want them to find me half naked and pull me out of the rubble from under you.
OMAR: What if you were on top? And what do you mean half naked? Only half?
LEILA: I'm going back under the bed and so should you.

> LEILA *grabs the baby and crawls back under the bed and* OMAR *follows begging.*

OMAR: Please. Okay, we can continue under the bed. It was my first choice anyway.
LEILA: Goodnight.
OMAR: Wait, I'm willing to accept the half-naked deal. Come on … Wait, we can do things fully dressed too you know. Leila … Leila …
LEILA: I said goodnight.

SCENE TWO

Street. Two armed GUARDS *are manning the checkpoint. They are dressed in civilian clothes and their faces are concealed behind a scarf.* MOHAMED *enters from the opposite side, his rifle slung across his shoulder, but he sees* SALMA *arriving at the checkpoint, so he hides out of view and watches her exchange with the* GUARDS. SALMA *is wearing conservative clothes and a hijab.*

GUARD 1: Papers.

> SALMA *hands the* GUARD *her passport. He looks at it and reads her name with a smirk.*

Salma MoheeDein. Salma … Salma … Salma … Where have I heard that name? Hey … [*To* GUARD 2] *This* is Salma.

> GUARD 1 *checks her out head-to-toe.* GUARD 2 *steps forward and does the same. They start to circle around her.*

GUARD 2: Well … hello, Salma. We've heard so much about you. Word has it you are really good at boosting the fighters' morale.

SALMA stands defiant seemingly unintimidated by the two men.

SALMA: I'm here to visit my brother Omar MoheeDein.

GUARD 1: Sure, but I think first ... you need to pay us a visit, no?

GUARD 2: Yeah, or are we not good enough for you?

SALMA: Mohamed Najjar will enjoy cutting off your tongues for speaking this way to me. Now let me through.

GUARD 1: Mohamed Najjar wouldn't give a rat's ass about someone like you.

The men laugh and tighten their circle around her.

SALMA: Then call him. What, are you too chickenshit? Call him.

GUARD 2: Okay. Fine. I'll call him.

GUARD 2 takes out his phone and dials. MOHAMED's phone rings. He is startled by the sound and quickly takes out his phone to switch it off, but it is too late—the GUARDS and SALMA have discovered his hiding spot and are looking straight at him. Awkwardly, he walks towards them.

MOHAMED: Is there trouble here?

SALMA is furious. She whispers to him.

SALMA: Mohamed? You were just standing there? Watching? Why? What were you thinking?

MOHAMED: [*dragging her aside*] I was thinking how I've heard so much about your power of persuasion with fighters I thought I'd see for myself how far you'd go with these scumbags—

SALMA slaps him on the face. He doesn't flinch. The GUARDS look at each other and smile, amused.

Why did you come back?

SALMA: To see Omar.

MOHAMED: Why?

SALMA: He is my brother.

MOHAMED: Yeah. Right. What's in it for you?

SALMA: Excuse me?

MOHAMED: What's in it for you?

SALMA: Is this an interrogation?

MOHAMED: Call it what you want. I'm responsible for protecting people here.

SALMA: From unarmed women? Well, you're certainly doing a good job, aren't you?
MOHAMED: You're not unarmed. Your tongue is a weapon of mass destruction.
SALMA: Are you done?
MOHAMED: No. What business do you have here?
SALMA: My business is none of your business.
MOHAMED: And you'd better keep it that way. [*To the* GUARDS] Let her pass.

> SALMA *starts to walk away, but stops and turns back to* MOHAMED.

SALMA: Wait. Mohamed, I heard about your mother. I'm sorry. She was a good woman.
MOHAMED: She was. She gave up her food portions to feed everyone else.
SALMA: I'm sorry she didn't make it. She was like a mother to me. I remember when she used to—
MOHAMED: [*interrupting*] Listen, you don't need to pretend to care about my family or my life. I'll protect you because I promised Omar I would. So save this crap, this emotional manipulation, for some other fighter. [*To* GUARD 1] Escort her to Omar MoheeDien's house.

> SALMA *stands still.*

[*Yelling*] *Go! Leave!*

> SALMA *walks away with the* GUARDS. MOHAMED *is left alone. He takes some hash out of his pocket and begins to prepare the sheesha. The* PIANO MAN *pushes his piano onstage and plays a sombre tune.* MAJID *and* OMAR *arrive. The three men nod at each other and sit down. They share the sheesha while they scroll on their smart phones. The* PIANO MAN *stops the music and exits.*

SCENE THREE

MAJID: *Yes! Yes!*

> OMAR *and* MOHAMED *give him a side glance and get back to their phones.*

I said *yes!* Hello …? Don't you want to know what happened?
MOHAMED and OMAR: [*together*] No.

MAJID: You jealous bastards.
OMAR: Just because she said, 'My heart is with you', it doesn't mean she is ready to marry you. Westerners say this shit to people like us all the time.
MAJID: How did you know she said that?
OMAR: I'm reading your Facebook thread.
MAJID: I think it's more than that. I think she really likes me. She likes all my photos and statuses. She shares all my posts.
MOHAMED: [*sarcastically*] You must have swept her off her feet. We have so much to learn from you, Romeo.
OMAR: First lesson: Private message your target Western female a thousand 'hello ... hello ... hello ... hello ... hello ... hello ...' and if this doesn't work, bring out the big guns with 'How are you? How are you? How are you?'
MAJID: How do you know I did that?
OMAR: I'm guessing.
MAJID: Well, my persistence paid off. I think she has fallen for me!
MOHAMED: Are you for real?
MAJID: Why wouldn't she fall in love with me?
OMAR: You are unemployed.
MAJID: I am a self-employed artist.
MOHAMED: You take photos of dead people on your phone.
MAJID: I document the impact of war.
OMAR: You and almost everyone else here. Seems our university degrees were the first casualty of war. Now everyone is either a blogger, a photographer or a fighter.
MAJID: Yeah, well, not everyone is an artist.
MOHAMED: If you're an artist, I'm an astronaut for the space shuttle program.
OMAR: *That* you are my friend. You get us high on the moon every day ... except today ... What is wrong with this stuff? I'm not even getting a hint of a buzz.
MAJID: Yeah ... this is shit. Where did you get it?
MOHAMED: Salim.
OMAR: Why didn't you get it from AbuKeef? His stuff is always good.
MOHAMED: Abukeef lost his head.
MAJID: Anger?
MOHAMED: Sword.

OMAR: Ouch!
MAJID: Poetic justice, if you ask me. The man spun our heads for years.
OMAR: How will we survive without his good hash? Soon we'll all be at each other's throats.
MOHAMED: So true. The fighters already miss him. Last night the shooting was so intense, it was clear everyone was on edge.
MAJID: I noticed. You only took short breaks in between the fighting.
OMAR: Too short. Hardly enough time for a man to get anything done.
MOHAMED: [*to* OMAR] Please allow me to apologise if our shooting at the enemy to protect your home and family interrupted your nightly routine with the wife. Next time tell us when you're horny, so we can hold fire long enough for you to complete the job.
MAJID: A real man is able to function even as the bombs fall.
OMAR: [*to* MAJID] Hey, lose your virginity first, and then you can tell me what real men can do.
MAJID: Why the hell did they behead AbuKeef?
MOHAMED: Just part of the routine. Take control of a village. Herd the men into the main square. Behead those guilty of vice and sin.
MAJID: Shit. We're next in line.
MOHAMED: Hopefully we'll be on the boat before they take over this place. I am a resistance fighter, I'm sure they have a sword waiting for me.
OMAR: Not necessarily a sword. If the army gets here first, you'll have an exquisite torture dungeon instead.
MAJID: Either way, you need to get out fast, and so do I.
OMAR: Or, here is an idea—you both stay with me and we fight like men.

> MAJID *and* MOHAMED *laugh.*

What's so funny?

> MAJID *and* MOHAMED *make bleating sounds.*

MOHAMED and MAJID: [*together*] Baaaa … baaaa …
OMAR: Cut it out, you two. I am capable of killing if need be, especially when it is to defend my home and family. Seriously. Just shut up.
MOHAMED: Don't romanticise this, brother. You really should just come with us. You should abandon this hellhole.
OMAR: *This* coming from the leader of the local resistance?

MOHAMED: Somewhere along the way, I've lost track of which resistance I'm fighting for. At the start, it used to be just us and them. Now there are so many others in the mix.
OMAR: Everyone who lives here is *us*. The rest out there is *them*.
MOHAMED: Yeah, but some of *us* are now fighting with *them*.
MAJID: And some of *them* are fighting with *us*.
MOHAMED: You see, there is our resistance, then there is their resistance, then there is the resistance to their resistance—
MAJID: [*interrupting*] Which claims to be the only legitimate resistance.
MOHAMED: [*sarcastically to* OMAR] Of course, you can have my vest and rifle when I leave. Try to kill at least one of theirs before they slaughter you.
MAJID: No. Omar will come with us.
OMAR: No way.
MOHAMED: Think of your wife and son. Trust me, you don't want them falling into their hands.
OMAR: I don't think putting the life of my family in the hands of people smugglers is a better option. Besides, I heard on the news that we're close to an agreement. Today's humanitarian passage was just the start.
MOHAMED: Don't believe the news. It is all propaganda. Take it from me, brother, I'm out there and I can see we're losing ground. *They* are advancing.
OMAR: Which 'they'? I'm a bit confused.
MOHAMED: The ones with the swords, the ones with the dungeons, and of course the ones with the fighter jets in the sky.
MAJID: [*feeling his neck*] I am terrified of swords.
OMAR: I prefer bullets. They're quick and easy, right?
MOHAMED: Sure. If you get one in your heart. But a month ago, Safwan got a bullet in his balls.
OMAR: Safwan has balls?
MOHAMED: He had a great pair, but they were always neatly tucked in his wife's pocket, no-one ever saw them.
MAJID: I don't know about you, but I prefer a beheading over a bullet in my man zone.
MOHAMED: Don't worry, no experienced sniper with the best of accuracy will manage to find your man zone.

OMAR: I guess you two prefer drowning?

MAJID: We're not going to drown.

OMAR: How do you know? So many are washing up on Europe's shores … men … women … babies …

MOHAMED: It is a calculated risk. A tactical necessity.

MAJID: [*looking at his phone*] Yes! Helen just private messaged me. Listen to this:

> *He reads the message imitating a sensual female voice while both* MOHAMED *and* OMAR *look at his phone screen.*

'My dear Majid. What happens to your people is heartbreaking. If there is anything I can do for you don't hesitate to ask. I want you to consider me a friend. Helen!'

OMAR: Maybe she fell in love with your profile pic.

MOHAMED: Show me. Wait a minute! I have a shirt and a pair of pants just like the one you're wearing in this photo.

OMAR: That's because he photoshopped his head on your body.

MOHAMED: What the hell is wrong with you? You can't just steal a friend's body without asking. I feel so … violated.

OMAR: Honestly, brother, we should warn the poor girl that you look like a monkey's ass.

MAJID: Screw you. I can't expect you to understand true love.

MOHAMED: True love? You would confess your love to a chimpanzee if she had a Western passport.

MAJID: Don't push me, Mohamed, or I swear I will tell Omar what you've been up to.

MOHAMED: I have nothing to be ashamed of.

OMAR: This hash is really shit. Let's just call it a night before one of you kills the other.

MOHAMED: Good idea.

MAJID: No, Omar, you should know this. I caught Mohamed surfing Australian gay dating websites.

OMAR: *What?* Why?

MOHAMED: It is not what you think.

OMAR: Then what is it?

MOHAMED: Look. I heard Australia, Canada and European countries give preference to persecuted minorities like Christians and the gays.

MAJID: So be Christian.
MOHAMED: My name is Mohamed.
OMAR: It doesn't sound like a gay name to me.
MOHAMED: Anyone can be a gay.
MAJID: No point challenging him. He'll read you the gay charter of rights.
MOHAMED: Just stay out of it, Majid.
MAJID: Sure. But when Helen and I get married and move to Canada, you and your Australian boyfriend can only visit us if you tell our kids that you are just friends. I don't want my future children to turn gay because of you.
MOHAMED: They won't turn into a gay. It is not contagious, you homo-fabric asshole.
OMAR: You mean *homophobic*?

> *They return to scrolling on their phones.* MAJID's *phone beeps. He looks at the incoming message with excitement.*

MAJID: Holy shit. These Western women are fast.
OMAR: Oh, yeah?
MAJID: You should read this stuff.

> MOHAMED *grabs* MAJID's *phone, and he and* OMAR *start reading the messages out loud.* MOHAMED *reads Helen's messages in a seductive female voice,* OMAR *reads* MAJID's *messages in an exaggerated masculine voice.*

MOHAMED: 'Dear Majid, I couldn't sleep last night. Are you okay?' Worried face.
OMAR: 'Yes, my dear Helen.' Relieved face. 'I am fine. The bombing was far from my house. Only our windows shattered, but we are all good.' Grinning cat face.
MOHAMED: 'Thank God. I was so worried. I think I may be growing attached to you.' Smiling cat face with heart eyes.
OMAR: 'To be honest, Helen, I have grown attached to you too. I don't want to scare you away but I think I'm falling for you.' Love heart.
MOHAMED: 'Why me?' Confused face. 'You are so handsome and many girls must want to be with you.'
OMAR: 'I only want one girl.' Love heart. 'You.' Love heart.
MOHAMED: 'I am not sure what to say. I wish you were here … with me.' Confused face.

OMAR: 'Would you marry me?'

MOHAMED: 'Yes.' Love heart. Kissing lips. 'We can raise our children by the lake … it will be so wonderful.'

OMAR: 'I wish I could touch you.' Eggplant emoji.

MOHAMED: 'I wish you could touch me. I'm breaking into a sweat just imagining your hands … on me … oh, Majid …' Hot lips.

OMAR: 'Why imagine? I will come to you. I must come to you. Would you like that?'

MOHAMED: 'I would love that. We should be together. I feel like you are my destiny. I'll call you on Skype soon. I want to wear something sexy for you.' Red love heart.

They hand the phone back to MAJID.

OMAR: Not bad, lover boy!

MOHAMED: Can we watch your steamy Skype call?

MAJID: No way. You're talking about my future wife. I am so happy. I'm sure she'll come to meet me in Europe, we'll get married and go to live in Canada … I can't believe how well this is going.

The men return to fiddling with their phones. MAJID'*s Skype rings.*

Oh, my God! This is her. That's her photo and name. How do I look?

OMAR: You look fine. Go on. Answer.

MAJID: [*fixing his hair before answering the call*] Hello, Helen. Helen? Helen?

OMAR: [*on his phone, imitating a female voice*] Hello, lover boy. It's me, Helen … I'm hot and ready for you.

MAJID: You sick son of a bitch. How did you hack into Helen's account?

OMAR: [*still using his sensual female voice*] I didn't. I am Helen. What … I'm not as sexy as you had hoped? I can change for you.

MOHAMED *is laughing hysterically.* OMAR *is puckering up his lips and sensually feeling his chest while* MAJID'*s anger explodes.*

MAJID: Why you … you … you … I'm going to kill you!

MAJID *jumps on* OMAR, *angry, and* MOHAMED *tries to stop him.*

OMAR: Don't worry, Mohamed, this is just a lovers' quarrel.

MOHAMED *pulls* MAJID *away from* OMAR. MAJID *is so angry. He storms off, yelling at* OMAR *as he goes.*

MAJID: You stupid selfish shithead! Did you think of how much of my time you've wasted?! Now I have to find someone else! How could you do this?!
OMAR: It was a joke. Majid … Majid …
MOHAMED: Let him go. He'll cool off. That was a good prank. My deepest respect to the master.

   Pause.

By the way, I saw your sister. She seems well.
OMAR: [*sighing*] Salma always lands on her feet.
MOHAMED: Sometimes she lands on other people's feet and crushes them.
OMAR: Will you ever forgive her?
MOHAMED: I don't care about her. Forgiveness is something you offer those you care about. Why did she come back anyway? What's left for her here?
OMAR: Us.
MOHAMED: I never pegged her for a woman who would give a damn about family.
OMAR: She's my sister, Mohamed. Be nice.

SCENE FOUR

Leila and Omar's kitchen/living room. There is a table, a sink, a few chairs and a sofa. SALMA *is sitting at the kitchen table looking at her phone.* LEILA *is changing Marwan's nappy on the sofa. The nappy is made up of towels and duct tape.*

SALMA: Is Omar avoiding me?
LEILA: Of course not.
SALMA: I haven't seen him since I got here. Where is he?
LEILA: He went out to get some water.
SALMA: But I brought water.
LEILA: He doesn't know that.
SALMA: Right.
LEILA: We have lots of funerals to go to today.
SALMA: Are you going to change?
LEILA: I did.

SALMA: Oh! I can never tell the difference anymore … we go from one shade of black to another.
LEILA: [*sighing*] I can't remember the last time I left the house in red or pink.
SALMA: Leila. I've noticed.
LEILA: What?

> LEILA *picks up Marwan and gently rocks him to sleep.*

SALMA: I thought you're not supposed to get pregnant while still nursing?
LEILA: Oh … that …
SALMA: [*smiling*] Congratulations. Another rascal like my brother is on the way. God help us all. Is Omar excited about this?
LEILA: He doesn't know. I don't know how to tell him.
SALMA: What?
LEILA: We can barely feed Marwan. Omar's teaching salary stopped when the school was bombed six months ago and we've spent all our savings since. There was a time when even buying water was by the gram … like we were buying gold.
SALMA: I can help with the money. That's why I'm here. To help.
LEILA: I know, but …
SALMA: You have to tell him. Hasn't he noticed—?
LEILA: He thinks I'm reacting to the war.
SALMA: It is a war … not an allergy.
LEILA: Yeah, well, I wish there was a pill for it.
SALMA: Funny you should say that, I have a whole range.
LEILA: I'm sure you do.
SALMA: I wouldn't survive without my happy pills.
LEILA: Your happy pills can't be working too well. You always look so miserable.
SALMA: I have a loose definition for the word 'happy'.
LEILA: Salma, thank you for coming back.
SALMA: What else was I to do? My husband is dead … his village … well, there is not much left of it … just piles of rubble and pillars of steel. Besides, being on my own, a woman in this madman's world was challenging to say the least. I needed to be around family. I need to be with you and Omar.

> *Pause.*

More importantly, coming here is another step closer to getting *there*.

LEILA: And where is *there*?
SALMA: *There* … is where hope lives. Across the sea that separates *us* from *them*. Life waits for us on the other side and I can't go there without you and Omar.
LEILA: On a boat?
SALMA: Yes. It's the only way we can do it. I've arranged for our transport to the coast. We could all leave tomorrow. Before the humanitarian corridor closes again.
LEILA: Really? Thank God! Thank you. But … how do we convince Omar?
SALMA: Leave him to me.

> LEILA *hands Marwan to* SALMA *and goes into the bedroom.* SALMA*'s phone rings.*

Yes, this is Salma.

> *Pause.*

What? You did what? No no no … that's not what we agreed on. I told you I draw the line at fourteen.

> *Pause.*

She's too young—

> *Pause.*

No … no … no … not her … I'm trying to help women, not …

> *Pause.*

Her father … I can't believe her father would … Listen, you are my client, you can't bypass me like this … You can't speak to the family directly … That's not what I agreed to do for you. It's not about the money … You have no idea what …

> LEILA *returns from the bedroom, and* SALMA *quickly terminates the call.*

LEILA: Are you okay? Did the sleazebag want a young girl? How old is he?
SALMA: It doesn't matter. He'll get what he wants. We've reached the bottom and there are plenty of bottom feeders here. They know that parents are now desperate, they'd rather marry their daughters young than watch them starve to death, or worse, see them captured by the savage warlords.

LEILA: *Ya allah!* Until when?

Disturbed, she sits down.

How do you do this?

SALMA: [*dismissively*] Don't be a drama queen.

LEILA: A drama queen? Salma, your clients are dirty old men looking for poor little girls to sexually exploit under the respectable guise of so-called marriages.

SALMA: Most of the ones I deal with are good men who genuinely want to help.

LEILA: Oh, stop it. Good men give charity without expecting a sex slave in return.

SALMA: What I do saves lives. If you have better ideas, please let me know. How else do we save these girls?

LEILA: Is that what helps you sleep at night?

SALMA: What helps me sleep at night is knowing I'm keeping my brother's family fed, so don't you dare question what I do. Does Omar know I give you money?

LEILA: I told him last night after you called. We had a huge fight about it.

SALMA: Wow! He must think very little of me.

LEILA: No, it's more the 'I'm a man' thing, you know. He would feel disgraced if he relied on his sister's help.

SALMA: I see. So you lied. The goody-two-shoes Leila lies to her husband.

LEILA: Oh, shut up. I hate lying to him. And I wouldn't accept anything from you if it weren't for Marwan.

SALMA: Of course, I know you only accept my help for your son's sake. Otherwise you would rather ride with Omar on your high horses all the way to your graves.

LEILA: Well, it's hard to stomach some of the marriages you've arranged … The last one I heard about, the man was fifty-five years old and the bride you provided was sixteen.

SALMA: I didn't provide her, she had a say in it and so did her parents. And he paid so much money the rest of her family had enough to pay for transport to get them far from here.

LEILA: What about the poor girl?

SALMA: If she plays her cards right, she will outlive the old man. She'll have enough money to live a grand life once the bastard is dead.

LEILA: Salma, have you ever gone younger than fourteen?
SALMA: Never.
LEILA: Swear it on Marwan's life.
SALMA: I said never … [*Whispering*] Not intentionally, anyway.
LEILA: What does that mean?
SALMA: It means nothing.
LEILA: Because if you ever go younger I would rather Marwan die of hunger than accept your money.
SALMA: We all have a magic line we draw between what is moral and what is immoral. That's fine. But take it from me, our morals are all relative to our needs. We can't all be perfect like Omar.
LEILA: No, we can't. Omar is a good man.
SALMA: And I am the wicked witch of the land? Look, Omar is an idealist. I love him for that, but I would never depend on him to survive, and neither should you.

SCENE FIVE

Funeral gathering. Everyone is dressed in black. In the centre of the room a WOMAN *sobs quietly while other* WOMEN *around her try to comfort her.* LEILA *and* SALMA *walk in, they are wearing long overcoats and hijabs. They shake the* WOMAN'S *hand and kiss her. Throughout this scene the* WOMEN *are whispering together the funeral prayer:*

WOMEN AT FUNERAL:
O Allah,
forgive and have mercy upon him,
Amen
excuse him and pardon him,
Amen
and make honourable his reception.
Amen
cleanse him with water, snow, and ice,
Amen
and purify him of sin.
Amen
Forgive our living and our dead,
Amen

those present and those absent,
Amen
our young and our old,
Amen
our males and our women.
Amen
Do not deprive us of his reward,
Amen
and do not let us stray.
Amen
Exchange his home for a better home,
Amen
and his family for a better family,
Amen
and his spouse for a better spouse.
Amen
Admit him into the Garden,
Amen
protect him from the punishment of the grave,
Amen
and the torment of the Fire.
Amen.

SALMA: I'm sorry. May he ascend to Paradise.

They sit down. SALMA *scans the room with her eyes, then whispers to* LEILA.

This funeral is a waste of my time. Not one young girl in this room? Where do they hide them all?

LEILA: [*whispering*] Omar was right when he said I should put you on a leash. You have no shame.

SALMA: My brother is full of shit.

Her phone rings to a dance tone. She awkwardly gets up and walks a few steps away. LEILA *gives her an annoyed stare.* SALMA *speaks in a low tone.*

Hello.

Pause.

Yes, this is Salma. What are you looking for?

Pause.

Yes, of course the girls I have look very young.

She looks around her to make sure no-one is listening.

I have a fourteen-year-old who looks much younger if you want, but you have to be serious about giving her a good life.

Pause.

I know others in this business offer short-term marriages, but I only take on clients who are serious about a lifelong commitment.

Pause.

How old are you?

Pause.

Wow! Are you sure you can ... you know ... handle a wife?

Pause.

How many wives do you have?

Pause.

Will she be living with any of them?

Pause.

Okay, good, as I said, I try to place the girls in the best environment possible.

Pause.

I will email you a few profiles you can choose from.

Pause.

Goodbye.

She returns to her seat next to LEILA. *She notices the* WOMEN *are staring at her.*

I am so sorry, aunty.

LEILA: [*whispering*] Can you not do this again?

SALMA: [*whispering*] It is business. I have to take these calls.

LEILA: [*to the grieving* WOMAN] We were just saying how devastating this must be ... May he rest in peace.

SALMA: May God avenge his death.
LEILA: He was loved by everyone.
SALMA: What a man ... so young and handsome.
LEILA: If I had a daughter, I would have wished for her to marry him.

> *The grieving* WOMAN *gives* LEILA *a sharp stare, but she doesn't notice.*

SALMA: All the girls prayed for just a glance from his beautiful eyes.

> LEILA *looks at the table and notices a framed photo of the deceased. She nudges* SALMA.

What?
LEILA: [*whispering*] I think we are at the wrong funeral. Look.

> SALMA *looks at the table and sees the photo.*

SALMA: This is not young Burhan.
LEILA: No. It is old Abu Yassin, that woman's husband.
SALMA: Oh, shit. [*Panicking*] And we told her all the girls were after him.
LEILA: Quick ... let's get out of here.
SALMA: [*to the grieving* WOMAN] We are so sorry for your loss. We must go now, we still have a few more funerals to catch.

SCENE SIX

Omar and Leila's kitchen/livingroom. The stage is dimly lit by a candle. LEILA *is lying on a mattress under the kitchen table, Marwan is sleeping next to her. She is stroking his hair and humming a lullaby.* OMAR *walks in from the bedroom, carrying a backpack. He is covered in rubble. He takes off his shoes. There are faint sounds of gunfire and explosions in the background.*

OMAR: All our official documents ... our entire life is now inside this backpack ... Leila?
LEILA: Under the table.
OMAR: Family photos, marriage certificate, Marwan's birth certificate, IDs ...

> *He looks around before he decides to place the backpack in the cupboard under the kitchen sink.*

I think this is a good place to keep them.

He takes off his dusty shirt and jeans.

Couldn't save anything else. The walls collapsed and the bed broke.

He chokes on the last word. Takes a deep breath and slides under the table next to LEILA. *He puts his arms around her.*

LEILA: It is a good time to remodel our bedroom.
OMAR: Well, the fighters seem to agree.
LEILA: Lots of open spaces now.
OMAR: So open our bedroom is practically a balcony.
LEILA: These war jokes never get old.
OMAR: No. No, they don't.

He buries his face in LEILA'*s embrace.*

LEILA: Marwan and I were in the kitchen. Our bedroom blew up while I was in the kitchen.

Pause.

This is the only part of our home left standing. Soon, we will end up like the piano man. Living in the street.

Pause.

Omar? What's the matter with you? Say something. Say something stupid. Please don't cry. Say anything.

OMAR *lifts his head, wipes a tear, and smiles sheepishly.*

OMAR: On the plus side, the piano man has been entertaining everyone in the street.
LEILA: That's my Omar.

She kisses him.

You were gone for a while.

OMAR: I couldn't find water. I'm sorry.
LEILA: Don't worry. Salma brought us some drinking water and some vegetables to cook tomorrow.
OMAR: Salma the saviour!
LEILA: You don't have to eat the vegetables or drink the water. But you have no right to starve Marwan and me.

Pause.

OMAR: I nearly died when I heard the explosion. I ran towards the house and I ...

> OMAR *and* LEILA *embrace. A complete silence hovers.*

The shooting stopped. Is Marwan sleeping yet?

LEILA: Almost. Oh, my God! You are sick. How can you be aroused? At this time? Really?

OMAR: I think it would be fun to try it down here.

LEILA: Fun?

OMAR: Yes ... When we slept under the bed it was so tight we couldn't ... do the important stuff.

LEILA: We didn't do *any* stuff, remember?

OMAR: That's what you think. In my head we did some wild things.

LEILA: Well then, what do you need me for? Just crawl back into your head.

OMAR: Never. Not when I have the real thing right here.

LEILA: I wonder if it is really better here?

OMAR: Of course, the space allows for a variety of positions.

LEILA: I meant better as in safer ... from the bombs.

OMAR: Not sure. But it is out of the way of sniper fire. More importantly, my love—the air is so much better here.

LEILA: [*sarcastically*] And the view is to die for.

> *Pause.*

Omar, I think we should put Marwan under the sink.

OMAR: What? Why?

LEILA: Today, at one of the funerals, the women were talking about how the only thing left standing from the Halaby home was some pillars and the kitchen sink.

OMAR: The Halaby home was a bigger house with a bourgeois sink.

LEILA: Well, our modest proletariat sink has enough room for a baby.

OMAR: Why not? If you think it is safer for him.

> *Pause.*

So ... is he sleeping yet?

LEILA: Not yet. Omar, many people are leaving now, before the UN corridor closes. Your friends are leaving too.

> OMAR *moves closer to her and strokes her arm.*

OMAR: Don't bring this up again. I told you, I will think about it.

Pause.

LEILA: I'm losing my mind. We're falling into a routine of funerals, hospitals, food rations, sleeping in unusual places, losing walls, losing friends, losing lives and limbs and carrying on like it is normal. Omar, our life is absurd.

OMAR kisses her neck.

You are trying to have sex with me the night our bedroom was bombed ...

OMAR: A: We agreed it was just remodelled. And B: I would try to have sex with you even if our bedroom didn't get bombed. Can't you see, this is the only normal we have?

LEILA: That's my point. Omar, they are almost here. We are surrounded by different militias and fighters and no-one gives a damn about us.

OMAR: I said I'll think about it.

LEILA: Promise?

OMAR: Promise.

Pause.

So ... is he sleeping yet?

LEILA: He might if you stop asking.

Silence lingers for a minute.

OMAR: Well ...

LEILA: What?

OMAR: Is he ...?

LEILA: You asked only a minute ago.

OMAR: It seems like an eternity.

LEILA: Patience.

OMAR: I don't want to miss out. We have to take advantage of this calm.

LEILA: Shhhh ...

Silence another minute.

OMAR: Is he sleeping?

Pause.

Leila? Leila ... please don't tell me you are asleep. Wake up ... just a little longer. I promise to make it worth your while.

LEILA: Omar, I am exhausted.
OMAR: But I've got some moves that will make the tiredness go away.
LEILA: [*laughing*] Shhhh ... you'll wake him up.
OMAR: Ah ha! So he *is* asleep.

> OMAR *pulls* LEILA *under the blanket.*

LEILA: No ... no kissing ... We both haven't brushed our teeth or showered in days ... or weeks ... I can't remember
OMAR: I don't care.

> *Sounds of* OMAR *kissing* LEILA.

LEILA: I miss the days of beauty routines. Long baths ... facial masks ... waxing ...
OMAR: Speaking of which, can I ask you a personal question—am I stroking your legs or mine?
LEILA: You are nasty.
OMAR: It's just ... there is so much hair. You remind me of Aunty Fatima's goat.

> OMAR *and* LEILA *giggle and move under the blanket. Sound of a big explosion, followed by the baby screaming. They come out from under the blanket, frightened.*

Just one more minute ... the world couldn't give us just one more minute.

SCENE SEVEN

Street. The PIANO MAN *pushes his piano to the centre and begins playing a lively tune.* OMAR, MAJID *and* MOHAMED *arrive at different times, joining the* PIANO MAN *and singing along. When the song ends, the* PIANO MAN *pushes his piano to the side and carries a suitcase. He bids the men farewell and leaves. The three friends sit around the sheesha to smoke, phones in hand.*

MAJID: [*to* OMAR] Give me your phone.
OMAR: Why?
MAJID: Just give it to me for a minute.

> OMAR *hands over his phone.* MAJID *holds* OMAR*'s phone while looking at his own phone at the same time and smiles.*

Here. You can have your phone back. I just wanted to make sure you are not pretending to be Sophia, my new love interest. I happen to be chatting with her right now.

OMAR: Sophia? That was quick. When did you hook that one?

MAJID: She was always my Plan B.

MOHAMED: Sophia? Isn't she the angry feminist who always posts statuses in capital letters: 'FUCK COLONIALISM', 'FUCK PATRIARCHY' … I don't think she likes men.

OMAR: Then she'll definitely like Majid.

MAJID: I wouldn't push if I were you, Omar. Thanks to you I wasted a week on your imaginary Helen. So shut up and let me figure out my new escape plan. Also, not that it is any of anyone's business, but Sophia *does* like men. She was devastated last year when her husband passed away. She nearly died and had to be taken to hospital for a nervous breakdown.

MOHAMED: I remember that. But it wasn't her husband she was mourning, you moron. She was mourning the death of her poodle.

MAJID: That can't be true. She had hundreds of people writing messages of condolence on Facebook … She got more messages than I did when my parents were killed last year. She even wrote to me at the time saying, 'I share your heartache. I too have just lost a loved one' … Are you telling me she was comparing losing her dog with my losing my parents?

MOHAMED *and* OMAR *nod and laugh.*

OMAR: I'm going to miss you two.

MOHAMED: There is still time for you to change your mind and come along.

OMAR: And plunge into the unknown?

MAJID: Anything is better than this.

MOHAMED: So true. And you can always join your wife's family. I hear they are doing well in Sweden.

OMAR: That's what they tell Leila. They don't want her to worry. But her dad spoke to me this morning—they will be deported back.

MAJID: Why?

OMAR: Their asylum application was rejected. This is happening everywhere these days. Countries compete to make money in contracts to destroy and to rebuild our cities only to destroy them again, but no-one wants the 'human flood of refugees' who try to escape from these wars.

MOHAMED: So that's what we are? A 'human flood'? Where do people like us go? Where is my family supposed to go? We can't survive here. My mother died of hunger, my sisters are all on the way ... Where are we supposed to go?

OMAR: Heaven.

MAJID: Don't panic. We just need to have a secure plan. That's all, really. Find love. Get married. I will find a job doing anything ... washing dishes, cleaning floors ... I don't care.

MOHAMED: I just want to have a chance at living a normal life. I want my sisters to go back to school and to grow up to be something.

> MAJID *shoots* MOHAMED *a sarcastic smile.* MOHAMED *is a bit rattled by it but ignores him.*

OMAR: How much did you have to pay for your tickets?

MOHAMED: One thousand American dollars each. That's just for the boat ride, not the transport from here to the coast.

OMAR: So if Leila and I were to go, I would need at least two thousand dollars. I don't have that kind of money. I'm surprised you do.

MOHAMED: My father sold everything he had to get us all on that boat.

MAJID: [*sarcastically*] Really?

OMAR: Even if I sold everything, I wouldn't have enough.

MAJID: Well ... you don't need to sell everything ... Sometimes you only have to sell one thing ... Isn't that right, Mohamed?

MOHAMED: What the hell is that supposed to mean?

MAJID: You know damn well what it is supposed to mean.

MOHAMED: What are you on about?

OMAR: Mohamed, your family's house was destroyed and your family lives in a shelter under a bridge that is probably going to be the first to go when the airstrikes begin. What does your father possibly have to sell?

MOHAMED: He said he had assets.

MAJID: Why don't you just drop the bullshit?

> MOHAMED *pounces on* MAJID, *grabbing him by the collar.*

MOHAMED: I've had enough of you ... your sarcasm ... your insinuation. If you have something to say just be a man and say it.

OMAR: [*pulling* MOHAMED *away*] Mohamed. Easy. You're choking him.
MAJID: Don't pretend you don't know ...
MOHAMED: Don't know what? Speak.
OMAR: Mohamed, his face is turning blue. You'll kill him.
MOHAMED: Speak.
MAJID: Go home and count your sisters. See if any one of them is missing.

> MOHAMED *storms out with his rifle in his hand.* MAJID *tries to catch his breath.*

MAJID: Shit. *Shit*. What have I done? Wait, Mohamed ... don't do anything stupid. We're supposed to leave in a few hours. Mohamed ...!

> MAJID *runs after* MOHAMED. OMAR *stands confused.*

SCENE EIGHT

Omar and Leila's kitchen/living room. LEILA *and* SALMA *are setting the table for dinner.* OMAR *walks in. He smiles when he sees* SALMA.

OMAR: If it isn't the matchmaker ...

> *He hugs* SALMA *and kisses her on her cheeks.*

Now shoo away ... we have no brides for you. This beautiful woman is taken.

> *He kisses* LEILA *on her forehead.*

> *The three of them sit at the table. There is sporadic gunfire in the background.*

SALMA: [*to* OMAR] Why aren't you eating? These are really good eggplants.
LEILA: Don't worry about him, Salma. He prefers the herb soup.
OMAR: I also don't like eating in the bedroom.
SALMA: That's right, you sleep here now.
OMAR: Where is Marwan?
LEILA: Napping under the sink.
SALMA: And under the stars.
LEILA: Salma brought a bunch of glow-in-the-dark star stickers and decorated the space under the sink so it looks like the ceiling in his bedroom.
OMAR: She is a good aunty ... sometimes.

SALMA: I heard on the news the coalition is planning airstrikes. This entire area could be wiped out.
OMAR: You've always been a bearer of good news, sis.
LEILA: Omar, you promised me to think about it. Tonight could be our last night here if we leave with Salma and the others.
OMAR: [*surprised*] Salma is leaving?
SALMA: Yes.
OMAR: You didn't even consult with me.
SALMA: Oh ... so now you're going to play the brother card? I don't need to consult with you.
OMAR: Of course not. You do as you please. You always do as you please.
SALMA: I'm not going to argue with you. In fact, I'll humour you. My dear brother, I would like your permission to leave ... again.
OMAR: You almost sounded convincing.
LEILA: Oh, grow up, you two.
SALMA: I'm sorry. Omar, I really think you should come with me.
OMAR: I'm not convinced leaving is a better option. Things might calm down here soon.
LEILA: And if they don't? Think of our son.
OMAR: You don't think I'm thinking about my son? You want me to put him on a boat that might sink?
SALMA: We have to weigh the risk. Staying here is high risk. Listen, I've checked the boat, it is solid.
LEILA: Omar, listen to me ... *they* are nearly here ...
SALMA: If we don't die by the swords we will die by the coalition bombs.

Pause.

I have money ... I paid your share ...
OMAR: I don't want your money.
SALMA: But ...
LEILA: Omar, please listen to her.
OMAR: Salma. I don't want anything from you. Stop filling my wife's head with false hope.
LEILA: I'm not a child. I can think for myself.

The gunfire stops. They all listen intently to the silence.

SALMA: You hear this? The calm before the storm.
LEILA: The resistance is down. They will march in now, and this place will become a target for the airstrikes.

SALMA: It's going to go downhill from here. Leila, tell him.
LEILA: What? No. Salma, not now. Not like this.
SALMA: Tell him. It might convince him to leave.
OMAR: What? Are you keeping something from me?

> LEILA *hesitates.*

What?
LEILA: I'm pregnant.

> *Pause.* OMAR *freezes for a moment, then his face lights up.*

OMAR: Thank God for this blessing. Why didn't you tell me?
SALMA: You need to look after your family. You need to leave with me. Do it for Leila, for your children—Marwan and the one on the way.
LEILA: Omar, I can't be pregnant, nursing and hungry in a war zone. I want to leave. There is no life here. Omar, I want to leave.

> OMAR *thinks for a minute, then shakes his head, signalling yes.*
> LEILA *excited, kisses him and then kisses and hugs* SALMA.

Oh, thank you thank you thank you thank you … Oh, I can't believe it, finally … I'll start packing … How much can we take with us?
OMAR: Slow down, Leila … Only to the coast … I'll need to see the boat before I decide the rest.
SALMA: Small steps … that's all we can ask for!

> *Loud knocking on the door. They are all startled.*

MAJID: Omar, open up. Quick. It's me Majid.

> OMAR *opens the door and* MAJID *comes in looking nervous.*

I'm sorry, Omar. I shouldn't have told Mohamed. I thought he knew. Now I've really messed things up. Forgive me. Please forgive me.
OMAR: Knew what?
MAJID: Salma, you need to hide. Mohamed is on his way. He wants to kill you.
OMAR: Why? Salma, what did you do?
MAJID: She arranged a marriage between his baby sister Khadija and an old rich man.
LEILA: Khadija? I saw her last week. She was playing barefoot in the street. She's a child. Salma, tell me you didn't.

> OMAR *drags* SALMA *toward the door,* LEILA *tries to intervene and stop him.*

OMAR: You are disgusting. Get the hell out of my house.

> SALMA *screams.* LEILA *separates her and* OMAR *and stands in the middle.*

LEILA: Omar, stop. Stop. Let's find out what happened first?
OMAR: What did you do?
SALMA: I didn't mean for this to happen. I swear I didn't.
OMAR: Don't lie.
SALMA: I was trying to arrange a marriage for the older sister Sommaya, but when the father started to speak directly to the groom, he switched sisters at the promise of more money.
OMAR: You started this. You made the connection. You brought this disease here. I want you out of our lives. I want you out.
LEILA: Omar, just calm down.
OMAR: You are a disgrace. Your husband died a martyr for his country and you desecrate his name.
SALMA: My husband was a disgusting rat who wanted people to see him as a powerful hero. I'm glad he's dead and I hope he is burning in hell.
LEILA: Salma, don't make things worse.
SALMA: Worse? Than this?
OMAR: Don't play the victim. It doesn't suit you.

> MOHAMED *walks in, holding his rifle. He takes slow, deliberate steps. Everyone freezes. He points the rifle at* SALMA.

MOHAMED: Where is my sister? [*Louder*] Where is my sister?
MAJID: Mohamed, put the rifle down. We can work this out.
SALMA: It wasn't my fault. Your father did this.
MOHAMED: And I'm supposed to believe a whore like you?
OMAR: Don't call my sister a whore.
MOHAMED: Why don't you ask your sister how she managed to get out of her husband's village after he was killed?
SALMA: I was injured in a bomb explosion and they brought me out in an ambulance.
MOHAMED: Good story. But it is not the truth. Every fighter I've met knows your story.
MAJID: Mohamed. Stop it. There is no need for this.
OMAR: You'd better not be making this up because if you are I will kill you.

MOHAMED: [*to* SALMA] You think you would have survived a day if it weren't for me and my friendship with your brother? [*Yelling*] *I* protected you from all the fighters here, despite your whore reputation and what have you done to me? What have you done to my family?

SALMA: I didn't do anything and I am not a whore. Omar, listen to me. I am not a whore.

OMAR: What did you do?

MOHAMED: Your sister slept with a soldier who mans the checkpoint near her house. That's how she got out.

LEILA: Salma?

OMAR: No ... Salma ... No ... no ... no ...

SALMA: I flirted with him only to get food and water. Omar, believe me, I was so stupid and naïve, but I didn't offer myself to him. He forced himself into my house, and he raped me. When I fought him he slashed my face. None of you even asked why I have this scar on my face. None of you wanted to know. You all just want to bury your heads in the sand.

LEILA: Oh, Salma ...

SALMA: I knew when he left me bleeding that soon his friends will want to have their turn.

LEILA: Salma, no. Don't ...

OMAR: Enough! I've heard enough. Stop.

SALMA: I ran to the Red Cross clinic. They put me in an ambulance and drove me out of the village. I found a way to survive. [*Louder*] I survived! And now you all stand and judge me. Well, fuck you all.

MOHAMED: This doesn't justify what you did.

SALMA: [*to* MOHAMED] No? Well, what about what you do? You fight your wars with guns and bombs and you turn women's bodies into weapons of war, symbols of honour. And when we are conquered, you think that we're better off dead than alive. You think death washes away shame? The only thing that washes away shame is survival. [*To* OMAR] I didn't invent what I do. I only provide a service that makes people's lives a little bit better.

LEILA: How did you make life better for Khadija?

SALMA: Khadija wasn't my idea. [*To* MOHAMED] Your father believed that his decision might save the rest of the family. By offering the youngest daughter, he made enough money to get the rest of your sisters out. No parent should ever have to make these decisions, but here in the pit of despair, where parents bury their children every day, these are the choices we are forced to make—which child to sacrifice in order to save the rest.

MAJID: Mohamed, we might be able to find your sister. Put your rifle down. Let's talk this through. Salma, do you have the man's contact information?

SALMA: I do. I know his name, where he lives, I keep a work profile for all my clients.

MOHAMED: Give it to me.

SALMA: No. Your sister has already left. Let us leave first. Once we've made it to safety, I promise you I will help you find her

Pause.

MOHAMED: Don't kid yourself about making it to safety … For as long as my sister is with that man … you will never be safe.

MOHAMED looks at his rifle and then at OMAR. OMAR nods. MOHAMED hands OMAR the rifle, takes off his vest and leaves it next to the door. They embrace and MOHAMED exits.

MAJID: Well. This is goodbye. Wish me luck, brother. I will stay in touch. Forgive me and pray for us.

MAJID and OMAR hug and MAJID leaves.

OMAR: [*to* SALMA] So this is what you've become?

SALMA: This is what *we've* become. Desperate, terrified, so hungry we feed off each other … they turned us into this.

OMAR: No. Some of us hold on to our dignity, our values, our humanity.

SALMA: And this is why they don't survive. Omar, you won't make it here. Come with me. Please. You are my family. I paid for your transport. Please don't stay here. Leila, say something.

LEILA: You should go. I won't accept anything from you anymore. I will not lose any more pieces of myself to this fucked-up war anymore. May God help you on your journey and may he have mercy on us.

SALMA takes two steps toward the door before turning around and looking lovingly at OMAR and LEILA, her tears falling. She leaves, shutting the door behind her.

OMAR: I will miss you.

LEILA *wipes her tears. The airstrikes begin.* OMAR *drags the mattress under the kitchen table while* LEILA *throws the pillows there.* OMAR *checks under the kitchen sink.*

LEILA: Don't wake him up.

OMAR: I won't. I just wanted to see his face. He looks like an angel. Oblivious to all the madness around him.

They lay down on the mattress.

LEILA: So they are all leaving now. Can you imagine what is going through their minds?

OMAR: Hope. Dreams. Fear.

LEILA: I pray they make it to wherever it is they are destined to find their peace.

OMAR: Me too.

Pause.

You hear that?

LEILA: The sound of bombs falling?

OMAR: Not any bombs. That's the sound of the West marching in our sky to save us. These bombs they are dropping are spreading liberty, freedom, and democracy.

The airstrikes are louder and more frightening. LEILA *and* OMAR *huddle together.*

I love you.

LEILA: I love you too.

OMAR: Darling … would you be so kind as to share a freedom bomb with me?

The sound of bomb falling. Lights out.

SCENE NINE

Omar and Leila's kitchen/living room. Debris everywhere. Kitchen table is broken. Blood stains on the floor. Noise outside of people talking over each other.

MALE VOICE: [*offstage*] Miss … Miss … Wait … We've pulled out two bodies from the flat. There is no-one else left there. You shouldn't go in. Wait. Don't go in, the ceiling may collapse.

SALMA *walks into the destroyed home. She is maintaining a strong posture, tears streaming down her face. She steps over rubble and furniture parts. The kitchen sink is the only thing left standing. She kneels down, opens the cupboard door, and smiles through her tears.*

SALMA: Hey, handsome. Are you ready? There is a boat waiting for us.

She takes out the baby and notices the backpack. She grabs it and exits the room. Fade to darkness. The sound of waves gently rocking a boat. Voices of men and women are heard reciting a prayer.

VOICES: Our stories are written on water
        Washed up along the shores,
        Scattered on sand in foreign land
        So far away from home.
        Hope, wrap us in your mercy,
        Love, sustain us through this journey,
        Faith, guide us to compassion
        So we may survive.

THE END

www.ingramcontent.com/pod-product-compliance
Lightning Source LLC
Chambersburg PA
CBHW050028090426
42734CB00021B/3473